ENDANGERED ANIMALS OF THE OCEANS

WORLD BOOK

a Scott Fetzer company
Chicago
worldbook.com

J591.68
END

Staff

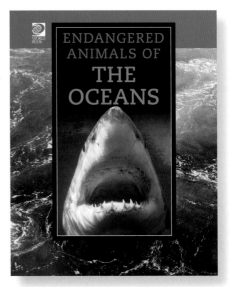

The cover image is the endangered great white shark.

World Book, Inc.
233 North Michigan Avenue
Chicago, Illinois 60601 U.S.A.

For information about other World Book publications, visit our website at **www.worldbook.com** or call **1-800-WORLDBK (967-5325).**
For information about sales to schools and libraries, call 1-800-975-3250 (United States) or 1-800-837-5365 (Canada).

Library of Congress Cataloging-in-Publication Data

Endangered animals of the oceans.
    pages cm. -- (Endangered animals of the world)
  Summary: "Information about some of the more important and interesting endangered animals of the oceans, including the animal's common name, scientific name, and conservation status; also includes a glossary, additional resources, and an index"-- Provided by publisher.
  Includes index.
  ISBN 978-0-7166-5627-2
  1. Marine animals--Juvenile literature. 2. Endangered species--Juvenile literature. I. World Book, Inc.
  QL122.2.E53 2015
  591.77--dc23

                                    2014020178

Endangered Animals of the World
ISBN: 978-0-7166-5620-3 (set)

Printed in China by Shenzhen Donnelley Printing Co., Ltd. Guangdong Province
1st printing October 2014

Contents

Why species in the oceans are threatened

The oceans cover nearly 71 percent of Earth's surface. These great bodies of water are so vast, that from the moon, Earth looks like a blue ball in the darkness of space. The continents divide Earth's waters into five major parts—the Pacific, Atlantic, Indian, Southern, and Arctic oceans.

The oceans are filled with an amazing variety of animal life—from microscopic *zooplankton* (tiny animals that drift near the surface) to gigantic whales. There are beautiful corals, sea urchins, and starfish. There are clams, squids, and other soft-bodied *mollusks* as well as shrimp, lobsters, and other hard-shelled *crustaceans*. More than 14,000 kinds of fish, including speedy tuna and ferocious sharks, travel the seas. Sea turtles, penguins, seals, and dolphins swim in the ocean, while albatrosses and other seabirds fly above it.

An estimated 720 *species* in Earth's oceans are threatened, many critically. (A species is a group of animals or plants that have certain permanent characteristics in common and are able to interbreed.) Of course, this number includes only those species known to science. Many species remain undiscovered. And almost certainly, a number of these animals are in peril or have even disappeared.

Threats. The oceans provide food, energy, minerals, and recreation. They also play a major role in Earth's climate system by regulating the air temperature and supplying the moisture for rainfall. If there were no oceans, life as we know it could not exist here.

Unfortunately, overfishing and other human activities have caused some marine species to become extinct—and continue to threaten many more. The fishing industry has harvested many kinds of fish faster than the fish stocks have replaced themselves.

Cities and other human developments near coasts have spewed industrial, agricultural, chemical pollutants; sewage; and garbage into ocean *habitats* (places in which an organism usually lives). Pollution poisons animals and depletes the water of oxygen. Some coastal habitats have been destroyed. Oil spills have polluted beaches, ocean waters, and the ocean floor. People continue to illegally dump other *toxic* (poisonous) materials into the sea.

Scientists warn that *climate change* (a warming of Earth's average temperature caused mainly by the burning of *fossil fuels* [coal, oil, natural gas]) is affecting marine *ecosystems*. (An ecosystem is made up of living organisms and their physical environment.) Threats include rising sea levels and an increase in acid levels in seawaters.

More than 5,000 ocean sites have been set aside by countries as marine protected areas to preserve sea life and habitats from human activities. But these areas cover less than 2 percent of the oceans.

In this volume. The species presented in this volume represent a variety of endangered animals in the oceans. From the smallest and simplest to the largest and most powerful, the oceans' wildlife is facing challenges from human beings.

Scientific sequence. The species are presented in a standard scientific sequence that generally goes from simple to complex. This sequence starts with *invertebrates* (animals without backbones) then moves through fish, reptiles, birds, and mammals.

Range. Red areas on maps indicate an animal's *range* (area in which it naturally occurs) in the oceans.

Glossary. Italicized words, except for scientific names, appear with their definitions in the Glossary at the end of the book.

Conservation status. Each species discussed in this book is listed with its common name, scientific name, and conservation status. The conservation status tells how seriously a species is threatened. Unless noted differently, the status is according to the International Union for Conservation of Nature (IUCN), a global organization of conservation groups. The most serious IUCN status is *Extinct,* followed by *Extinct in the Wild, Critically Endangered, Endangered, Vulnerable, Near Threatened,* and *Least Concern.* Criteria used to determine these conservation statuses are included in the list to the right.

Conservation statuses

Extinct All individuals of the species have died

Extinct in the Wild The species is no longer observed in its past range

Critically Endangered The species will become extinct unless immediate conservation action is taken

Endangered The species is at high risk of becoming extinct due to a large decrease in range, population, or both

Vulnerable The species is at some risk of becoming extinct due to a moderate decrease in range, population, or both

Near Threatened The species is likely to become threatened in the future

Least Concern The species is common throughout its range

Icons. The icons indicate various threats that have made animals vulnerable to extinction.

Key to icons

 Disease

 Hunting

 Global warming

 Overfishing

 Habitat disturbance

 Pet trade

 Habitat loss

 Pollution

Tridacna gigas

Conservation status: Vulnerable

The giant clam is the largest living *bivalve mollusk*. Mollusks are soft-bodied *invertebrates* (animals without backbones). They have no bones, though most have a hard outer shell that protects the body. Bivalves are mollusks with a shell made of two pieces, called valves. The valves are connected at one end with a hinge that allows the shell to open (when the animal feeds and breathes) and close (when the animal wants to protect itself). Other bivalves include clams and oysters.

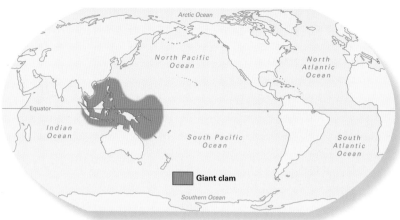

Appearance. The shell of the giant clam can grow almost 5 feet (1.5 meters) long. The weight of the animal can reach almost 660 pounds (300 kilograms). The shell of older giant clams is so thick and rough that it cannot close completely. Within the shell is the clam's mantle, the soft, fleshy part of the body. The giant clam's mantle is typically golden brown with many *iridescent* blue, purple, or green spots. (Iridescent objects change color depending on the angle from which they are viewed.) These spots increase in number as the clam ages. The mantles of the oldest giant clams may be all blue or purple.

Habitat. Giant clams may live for 100 years, but they never go anywhere. Like other clams, the giant clam remains attached to the sea floor as an adult. Such animals are said to be *sessile* (fixed to one place). Clams anchor themselves to the sea floor with a muscular organ called a foot. The giant clam lives mainly on shallow coral reefs and in tropical lagoons in the Indian and southwestern Pacific oceans.

Diet. Giant clams have a special relationship with single-celled algae known as *zooxanthellae*. These algae, which live in the clam's mantle, make food in a process called *photosynthesis*.

(In photosynthesis, plants and algae make carbohydrate food from carbon dioxide and water in the presence of light, releasing oxygen as a by-product.) The clam eats some of this food. In return, the clam gives the algae a safe place to live. This type of relationship between *species* (types)—in which both benefit—is called *mutualism*. The giant clam gets additional food by eating plankton that it filters out of the water.

Some people believe that giant clams can clamp down on human swimmers and divers to capture them and eat them alive. But no such attack has ever been proven. Furthermore, the adductor muscle that closes the giant clam's shell moves too slowly to catch a person by surprise.

Threats. The giant clam's existence is threatened by people who kill the clams to get the adductor muscle for food or the shells for ornaments, bowls, and other uses. The clams have also been captured alive to display in aquariums. In addition, the giant clam's coral reef *habitats* (living places) have been harmed by human activities, including fishing with dynamite, poisons, or bleach, and by various kinds of pollution. Because of these problems, giant clams have disappeared from some areas.

The shell of a giant clam may grow so thick and rough that it cannot close completely.

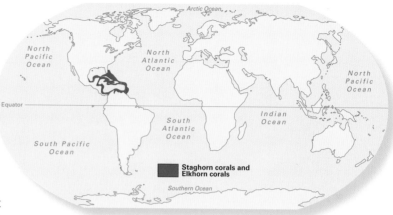

Corals are *sessile* (fixed) marine *invertebrates* (animals without a backbone) related to jellyfish and sea anemones. Individual coral animals—tiny tube-shaped organisms called *polyps*—live together in colonies. The polyps create hard, limestone *exoskeletons* (exterior coverings) around themselves. Corals create large formations known as coral reefs. Coral reefs are among the world's most *biologically diverse ecosystems*. That is, they host a wide variety of colorful fish and other sea animals in a particular environment.

Threats. Coral reefs are also among the most threatened ecosystems on Earth. Reefs are destroyed or damaged by certain fishing practices, by overfishing of reef animals, and in collisions with ships. Chemical pollution from farms and industries also harms the reefs.

Climate change (the warming of Earth mainly because of human activities) is another threat. Water that is too warm causes corals to *bleach*. That is, the golden-brown *zooxanthellae* (type of algae) that live in the corals' tissues turn white and die. Like giant clams, corals have a *mutual-*istic relationship with these algae, from which they obtain much of their food. When the algae die, so do the corals. And when the corals die, the entire reef ecosystem is put at risk.

Acropora corals are a *genus* (group of related species) of more than 100 corals that are especially sensitive to bleaching. Thousands of other marine organisms depend on the corals, which form the foundations of many reefs. Two seriously endangered species of *Acropora* are the staghorn coral and the elkhorn coral.

Staghorn corals have been damaged by a bacterial disease that destroys the corals' exoskeleton.

Populations of elkhorn coral, once the most common coral off the southern coast of Florida and throughout the Caribbean Sea, have fallen dramatically.

Staghorn coral
Acropora cervicornis

Conservation status: Critically Endangered

Staghorn corals are so named because the branches of their limestone colonies look like the antlers of a *stag* (male deer). These branches, which may grow 6.5 feet (2 meters) long, grow fast—up to 4 to 8 inches (10 to 20 centimeters) every year. Pieces of the branches that break off and fall to the sea floor may grow into new coral colonies.

Staghorn coral is found in warm waters in the Atlantic Ocean, Caribbean Sea, and Gulf of Mexico, from southern Florida to Venezuela. Populations of staghorn corals have collapsed since about 1980 for several reasons. Many have been affected by a bacterial disease called white-band disease, which destroys the coral's exoskeleton. Hurricanes, bleaching, and pollution have also harmed the corals.

Elkhorn coral
Acropora palmata

Conservation status: Critically Endangered

Elkhorn corals have thick branches that resemble the antlers of elk. The elkhorn branches grow to about the same length as the thinner staghorn branches. They can also grow into new colonies when they break off.

Elkhorn coral used to be the most common species of coral off the coast of southern Florida and throughout the Caribbean Sea. However—as with the staghorn coral—its populations have crashed since the early 1980's. White-band disease and the other problems facing staghorn corals also affect elkhorn corals.

Conservationists are working to save both these species, as well as other coral species, in a large protected area called the Florida Keys National Marine Sanctuary.

Heliopora coerulea

Conservation status: Vulnerable

Blue coral skeletons are a beautiful bluish-gray color. No other coral is this color. The skeletons of blue corals are made of a mineral called crystalline aragonite. That is the same mineral that makes up the shiny inner shells and pearls of some oysters. Blue corals are a type of coral known as a soft coral. By contrast, staghorn, elkhorn, and most other corals are known as hard corals—all of which have skeletons made from the mineral calcium carbonate (the scientific name for limestone). Blue coral skeletons form groups of blue-gray columns with short branches near the top.

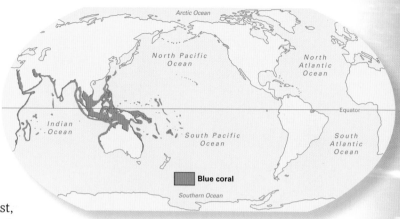

Blue coral

Coral colonies. Different kinds of soft coral colonies have different structures. Some colonies have no real skeleton. They are made of the corals' soft, tiny *polyps* (tube-shaped animals) connected with fleshy tissue—though there are hard, needlelike objects, called spicules, in the tissue. In blue coral colonies, the blue-gray skeletons have soft gray-white or olive green polyps sticking out of little holes in the aragonite. Each polyp has a mouth surrounded by eight tiny tentacles, which help the coral animal capture plankton and other food. In some colonies, polyps are so numerous that they completely cover the skeletons. For this reason, human divers usually never see the beautiful skeleton of this *species* (type).

Blue corals rely on more than their tentacles to get food. Like staghorn and elkhorn corals, they have a mutually beneficial relationship with the *zooxanthellae* (algae) that live in their tissues. These algae share food with the corals that the algae make through *photosynthesis* (energy-producing process), and the corals give the algae a safe place to live.

Reproduction. The polyps of blue corals reproduce by a process called brooding. Each polyp produces *larvae* (immature forms of the polyps) inside their bodies. After a period of development, the larvae are released into the water. Finally, these larvae settle on the outside of the colony or on the sea floor, where they develop into the adult polyps.

Habitat. Blue corals live in shallow ocean waters of the Indo-Pacific region. This region extends from the Red Sea and the waters of eastern Africa to the waters of Southeast Asia, Japan, and Australia. The largest-known colony of blue corals has been identified off Ishigaki Island in southwest Japan.

Threats. Many coral reefs in the Indo-Pacific region have been *degraded* (reduced in quality) or destroyed by human activities. Certain populations of blue coral have become rare in some areas, though they remain common in others. The threats facing reefs in the Indo-Pacific are similar to those that affect other coral reefs around the world—diseases, pollution, warming water, bleaching, and hurricanes.

Blue corals are especially threatened by collectors, who value the attractive skeletons for jewelry and ornaments. The corals are also collected for aquariums.

The massive blue skeletons of blue coral are usually hidden by green or blue coral polyps.

Coelacanth
Latimeria chalumnae

Conservation status: Critically Endangered

Sulawesi coelacanth
Latimeria menadoensis

Conservation status: Vulnerable

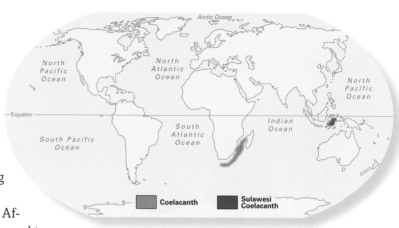

Imagine suddenly discovering a living dinosaur today. That's close to what Marjorie Courtenay-Latimer, a South African naturalist, did in 1938. She happened to see a fish called a coelacanth lying on a boat docked in East London, South Africa. The sight was shocking because scientists had thought that coelacanths had been extinct for 80 million years. The fish found by Courtenay-Latimer was identical to coelacanths known from fossils dating as far back as 360 million years ago.

Habitat. Since 1938, many coelacanths have been found, and scientists have identified two living *species* (types) of these primitive-looking fish. One species lives in the Indian Ocean off the coasts of South Africa, Mozambique, and Madagascar. Another species lives in the western Pacific Ocean off the Indonesian island of Sulawesi. Coelacanths are found in waters as deep as 2,300 feet (700 meters).

Appearance. Coelacanths are dark brown to bluish-gray fish that grow to more than 6 feet (1.8 meters) long and weigh up to 210 pounds (95 kilograms). Several features of the body are unique among living fish but known from fossilized fish. For one, coelacanths have muscular fins with bones—almost like legs—on the bottom of their body. Inside the skull, they have a special hingelike joint that allows the front part of the skull to swing upward. This makes the mouth open wider while the coelacanth feeds on fish, squid, and other sea animals.

Under the spinal cord, they have a hollow, fluid-filled *notochord,* a structure that early *vertebrates* (animals with backbones) had

hundreds of millions of years ago. Their back bones, called vertebrae, look as though they're not completely formed, compared with the vertebrae of other living animals.

Another strange feature of the coelacanth is a sensitive structure in the snout called the rostral organ. This organ can detect electric fields in the environment. Biologists believe that this ability may help the fish find prey and navigate around objects in its deep, dark surroundings. The fish hunt mostly at night. During the day, they often group together in undersea caves to rest.

Unlike most fish, the female coelacanth does not lay eggs. Instead, she gives birth to several fully formed young, known as pups. They are about 14 inches (36 centimeters) long at birth.

Threats. Biologists consider coelacanths to be important fish for the understanding of the evolution of land animals. Most biologists believe that coelacanths are similar to the fish that was the ancestor of four-legged animals. Unfortunately—after surviving for more than 360 million years—coelacanths may be in danger of extinction. Many coelacanths are accidentally caught and killed by people fishing for sharks, oilfish, and other fish species. Their populations are believed to be small. But the deep-sea *habitats* (living places) of coelacanths make it difficult for scientists to estimate their population sizes.

The coelacanth (shown in a museum display, top) and the Sulawesi coelacanth (above) are often called "living fossils" because scientists thought they became extinct 80 million years ago. The fish is now in danger of a modern extinction because of certain fishing practices.

Great white shark

Carcharodon carcharias

Conservation status: Vulnerable

The great white shark—the ultimate "jaws" of the sea—can grow to a length of more than 21 feet (6.4 meters). Unlike most other sharks, great white sharks are *warm-blooded*. That is, they can keep their body temperature higher than that of the cool seawater. Being warm-blooded helps them grow faster and stronger than most other sharks. These awesome animals live in coastal areas throughout the world.

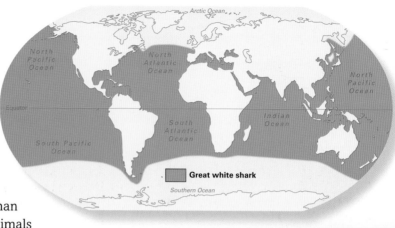

Threat to people. The great white shark is dangerous to people. Every year, some swimmers and surfers are attacked by great whites. These attacks are most common along the coasts of California and Oregon on the Pacific Coast of the United States, South Africa, and southern Australia. According to scientists, great whites attack human beings because—to the sharks—people look like their favorite food: seals and sea lions. The sharks make this mistake most often when people are swimming at the surface or floating on surfboards.

Some people die from great white shark attacks. But—amazingly—many attack victims survive, though they may be left with a serious bite wound. People are able to survive these attacks because of the way that great white sharks hunt their prey. A great white shark first stalks its prey from behind and beneath. It then suddenly takes one huge bite from the body. After this first bite, the shark typically waits for the victim to bleed to death before eating it. This wait allows the shark to avoid the claws and teeth of a struggling seal or sea lion. Fortunately for people, the delay gives human victims a chance to escape.

Another reason for the attacks on people is that great white sharks are more aggressive and energetic than many other shark *species* (types). Scientists on a research boat off the coast of South Africa experienced a frightening

demonstration of the shark's energy in July 2011. The researchers were throwing sardines off the boat as shark bait during a study of shark populations. Suddenly, a great white shark leaped out of the water and right into the boat—almost landing on a crew member.

The crew poured water on the stranded shark's *gills* to keep it alive until the boat returned to shore. (A gill is an organ in fish and other animals that absorbs oxygen from the water.) Then a crane was used to lift the 10-foot- (3-meter-) long fish out of the boat and release it back into the sea.

Teeth. The massive jaws of the great white shark have sharp, triangular teeth with jagged edges. About 300 teeth in several rows develop in stages. The front rows have from 50 to 80 functioning teeth. When a tooth in a front row is lost, a developing tooth from a back row moves forward and grows larger to take its place.

Threats. The global population of great white sharks has declined because of many decades of sport and commercial fishing. The fish are considered a highly prized trophy among sport fishers. High prices are paid for their teeth, jaws, and fins. Today, most catches of great white sharks are either accidental or illegal, because many countries have laws that protect the major populations of the species.

Earth's largest predatory fish, the great white shark can detect tiny amounts of blood in the water up to 3 miles (5 kilometers) away.

Sphyrna mokarran

Conservation status: Endangered

There are nine *species* (types) of hammerhead shark, which has a wide, flattened head shaped like the head of a hammer. One eye and one nostril are located at each end of the head. Tall, pointed *dorsal fins* (back fins) are another unusual feature. The smallest hammerhead is the bonnethead, which is about 5 feet (1.5 meters) long. The largest is the great hammerhead, which may reach about 20 feet (6 meters) long.

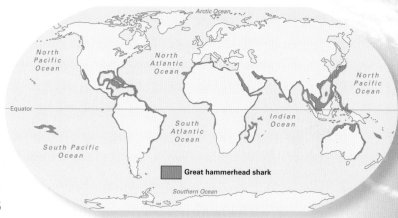

Great hammerhead shark

Head. Scientists have proposed several explanations for the strange shape of the head of these meat-eating sharks. The flatness of the head may help the sharks swim faster, because water flows over the head easily. The wide separation of the eyes may help the sharks scan wider areas of the ocean for food. The widely spaced nostrils may aid the animals in "homing in" on odor trails during their hunts.

Another benefit of the long head could be more space for sensing organs called ampullae (am PUHL ee) of Lorenzini. These organs are bundles of sensory cells located in small *pores* (holes) on the shark's head. The cells detect weak electric fields given off by other animals, as well as changes in water temperature and chemistry. The large number of ampullae of Lorenzini on their big head helps the hammerhead shark find fish, shellfish, and other prey.

Habitat. The great hammerhead shark lives in tropical and *temperate* waters (between tropical and polar regions) around the world. Hammerheads are most often seen near coral reefs and other places near the shore, though they also live in the open ocean far from shore. When tropical waters become too warm during summer, large groups of the sharks migrate to cooler waters. Some species of this shark live alone, but others form large schools.

Diet. Stingrays are one of the great hammerhead's favorite foods. The sharks avoid the stinging barbs of the rays by first pinning the dangerous animals to the sea floor with their hammers. The sharks then bite off the large "wings" of the rays so that the rays cannot move. Other animals eaten by great hammerheads include catfish, groupers, squids, crabs, and other sharks. Some great hammerheads are cannibals—that is, they eat other members of their species.

Threats. The great hammerhead shark is endangered mainly because it is killed for its large dorsal fins, its skin, its meat, and its liver oil. The fins are used to make shark-fin soup, which is especially popular in Asia. The skin is made into leather. The meat is used for food or to make "fish meal" (used as fertilizer and as feed for poultry). The liver oil is made into vitamin supplements. Commercial fishing operations sometimes kill great hammerheads accidentally when trying to catch other fish. Populations of the species have declined the most in the Gulf of Mexico and in the eastern and northwestern Atlantic Ocean.

The great hammerhead shark has one eye and one nostril at each end of its wide, flattened head.

Rhincodon typus

Conservation status: Vulnerable

The largest living fish, the whale shark grows to a length of at least 40 feet (12 meters) and a weight as great as 14 tons (12.5 metric tons). These giant fish live in tropical and *temperate* (between polar and tropical) ocean waters across the world but are most common in the tropics. Whale sharks are also unique in other ways. They are dark grayish-blue to reddish-brown with large, white-yellow spots on the upper side of the body. Their head is wide and flat, with a mouth that stretches almost as wide as the body. Several large *gill* slits (openings for breathing organs) are on the sides of the head.

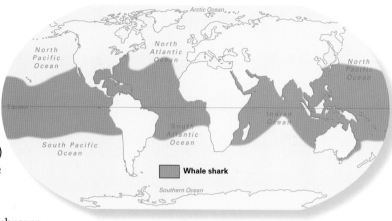

Eating. The wide mouth of a whale shark contains hundreds of tiny, hooked teeth. However, whale sharks do not bite or chew their prey.

Rather, the mouth works like a gigantic vacuum cleaner—sucking in plankton, small fish, and shellfish. The sucked-in water passes through the mouth and out the gill slits, but the small animals become trapped in filterlike structures made of *cartilage* (tissue that is softer and more flexible than bone) that are located under the gills. The shark then swallows the animals.

The whale shark is the largest living fish. Despite its size, it poses no threat to human beings.

Diet. Whale sharks can be seen both near the shore and far offshore in the open sea. They are usually alone, but groups with more than 100 individuals have also been observed. Large groups of whale sharks gather in areas that have a lot of plankton and other food. These groups tend to travel with schools of fish that eat the same kinds of food. The groups typically revisit these food-rich areas on a regular basis, making those sites popular attractions for tourists who want to see the whale sharks. Scientists have tracked some whale sharks traveling for many hundreds of miles (kilometers) as they roam through the sea.

Despite their great size, whale sharks are gentle giants that pose no threat to humans. Snorkellers have reported being close to whale sharks and watching as the big fish ignored them and slowly swam away. Scientists have studied some whale sharks in huge aquariums in Japan, also noting the shyness and gentleness of these supersharks.

Threats. In some countries, including Taiwan and the Philippines, whale sharks are hunted for food. Their meat and fins—used for shark fin soup—are sold for high prices. The sharks are also captured for their liver oil and cartilage, which are used to make health supplements and traditional Chinese medicines. Another problem for whale sharks is that boats sometimes ram into them.

Whale sharks have benefitted from their popularity as *ecotourist* attractions in areas that the sharks visit every year, such as the northwest coast of Australia. The Australian government enforces strict guidelines for these shark-watching tours to make sure that the animals are not harmed by tour boats or the activities of the tourists.

Sawfish

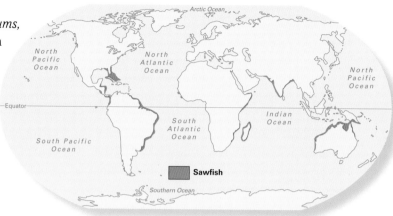

Sawfish have long snouts, called *rostrums,* that look like saw blades. The rostrum is lined with sharp scales that resemble the teeth of a double-sided saw. Sawfish use the rostrum to dig into the mud of the sea floor for fish, *crustaceans* (hard-shelled animals), and *mollusks* (soft-bodied animals). They also swipe the rostrum from side to side as they swim through schools of fish, stunning or stabbing their prey.

Body. Sawfish are a type of ray, fish related to sharks. Instead of bone, the skeleton of a sawfish is made of *cartilage* (soft, flexible tissue). The sawfish's body combines the flattened shape of most rays and the torpedo shape of most sharks. The largest sawfish are approximately 25 feet (7.6 meters) long.

Habitat. Sawfish live in warm ocean waters, mostly near shorelines. Some *species* (types) also enter river systems and lakes. Unlike many sharks, which must swim to breathe (so that oxygen-containing water flows into their *gills* [breathing organs]), sawfish can breathe while lying still on the ocean bottom. They have special pumping muscles that draw water into their gills.

Threats. All seven *species* (types) of sawfish are in danger of extinction. The fish are killed for their rostrums and fins, which can be sold illegally for large sums of money. Body parts are used for food or traditional remedies, or to make collectible items. Fishers often catch sawfish accidentally. Because of the sawfish's critically endangered status, international law bans their capture and the trade in their body parts.

The sawfish's sawlike snout, called a rostrum, is lined with sharp scales that resemble teeth.

Two sawfish species are native to the waters of the United States—the largetooth sawfish and the smalltooth sawfish. These species are endangered, in part, because human developments have destroyed the vegetated coastal *habitats* (living places), such as mangrove forests, where young sawfish live.

Largetooth sawfish
Pristis pristis
Conservation status: Critically Endangered

The rostrum of this species has from 14 to 23 large "teeth" on each side. Largetooth sawfish used to be common in U.S. waters from Texas to Florida, but they have not been seen there since the mid-1900's. They are still found along the northern coasts of Central and South America, the northwestern and northeastern coasts of Africa, the coast of India, and the waters around Indonesia and Australia. In addition, they are more likely than most other sawfish to be found in rivers and lakes. Many of these fish

A scientist releases a sawfish that has been tagged so its position can be tracked by researchers.

live in Lake Nicaragua in western Nicaragua, where they were formerly caught commercially.

Smalltooth sawfish
Pristis pectinata
Conservation status: Critically Endangered

The rostrum of this species has 23 or 24 small "teeth" on each side. The smalltooth sawfish used to live in U. S. waters from Texas to Florida and up the Atlantic Coast to North Carolina, but today it remains only in Florida. Elsewhere in the world, it is found mainly in the Atlantic waters of Central America and northwestern Africa. According to some scientific estimates, the population of the smalltooth sawfish has declined by at least 95 percent since the mid-1900's.

Tuna are fast and fierce ocean fish with torpedo-shaped bodies. They are among the most popular food fish in many countries, and their fighting ability makes them popular sport fish. Unfortunately, their popularity has led to overfishing, and they are now endangered.

The overfishing of tuna has also put dolphins at risk. In a fishing method called *purse seining*—the chief method for catching tuna—large nets are used to encircle the fish. Many dolphins have been killed when they became accidentally trapped in these nets. Laws in some countries now require purse seine nets to have openings for dolphins to escape. Some laws also ban the purchase of tuna caught in nets that kill dolphins.

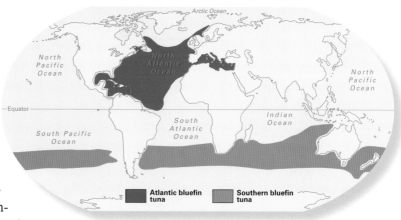

Atlantic bluefin tuna
Thunnus thynnus
Conservation status: Endangered

The Atlantic bluefin tuna is the world's largest tuna, growing to as much as 14 feet (4.3 meters) long and weighing up to 1,600 pounds (730 kilograms). The fish reaches this size by almost constantly eating small fish, shellfish, squids, and other animals. This tuna's body has a striking coloration, with a metallic blue top and a silvery-white bottom.

The tuna's body is perfectly streamlined—meaning that water can flow over it smoothly and easily, with little resistance. This allows the fish to zip through the sea at speeds as fast as 45 miles (72 kilometers) per hour. Like other tuna—and unlike most fish—the bluefin cannot pump water over its *gills* (breathing organ). Thus, it cannot get oxygen from the water unless it keeps swimming. Most sharks have to keep swimming for the same reason.

Like the great white shark, the Atlantic bluefin tuna is *warm-blooded*. That is, the tuna can keep its body temperature steady, regardless of the temperature of its surroundings. Every year, schools of Atlantic bluefin tuna migrate the vast distances between the cold waters off Newfoundland and Iceland and the warm waters of the Gulf of Mexico and the Mediterranean Sea. They *spawn* (lay eggs) in the warm waters.

Southern bluefin tuna
Thunnus maccoyii
Conservation status: Endangered

During most of the year, the southern bluefin tuna lives in the cool ocean waters of the Southern Hemisphere. There, like Atlantic bluefin tuna, southern bluefin tuna feed on fish, shellfish, squids, and other animals. However, during spawning season, these fish migrate to tropical waters between Indonesia and western Australia.

Females do not spawn until they are about 8 years old. After hatching, the young stay in schools in shallow coastal waters until they are about 5 years old. They then swim out to the open ocean. Members of this *species* (type) can live for 40 years.

The high fat content of southern bluefin tuna has made their meat very popular in Japan for a raw-fish dish called sashimi. A single southern bluefin tuna can sell for thousands of dollars in Japan.

The Southern bluefin tuna (left) and the Atlantic bluefin tuna (below) are swift, fierce fish whose meat is a popular food in many countries.

Lepidochelys kempii

Conservation status: Critically Endangered

The most seriously endangered marine turtle, the Kemp's ridley sea turtle, is also the smallest of the seven sea turtle *species* (types). It grows to a length of about 28 inches (71 centimeters) and reaches a weight of about 100 pounds (45 kilograms). The species is named after Richard Kemp, a Florida fisher who in 1906 was the first person to recognize this turtle as a unique species.

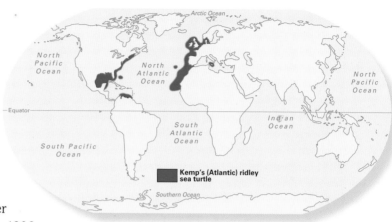

Kemp's (Atlantic) ridley sea turtle

Habitat. Like other sea turtles, the Kemp's ridley lives almost its entire life in the ocean. Females normally return to land only to lay eggs. Most males never return to land. Kemp's ridley sea turtles live in the Gulf of Mexico and along the Atlantic seaboard of the United States, where they eat crabs, jellyfish, *mollusks* (soft-bodied animals), fish, and seaweed.

Reproduction. Sometime around May of each year, large groups of these turtles begin to gather together off a beach near Rancho Nuevo, Mexico. Repeated waves of females then come ashore to lay their eggs on the beach. This mass arrival of female sea turtles is known as an *arribada,* the Spanish word for *arrival.* Rancho Nuevo is the largest nesting site for Kemp's ridleys, but this species also nests on other beaches in the Gulf region.

Scientists are not sure how all the females manage to arrive on the beach at roughly the same time. Some scientists think that the females release chemical cues known as *pheromones,* which call them together. Other scientists think that offshore winds or phases of the moon may influence the turtles' behavior.

The Kemp's ridley is the only sea turtle that nests mainly during the daytime. The female lays about 100 leathery, white eggs in a hole she digs in the sand with her hind flippers.

She covers the hole with sand and then returns to the sea. After the eggs hatch, in about 50 to 70 days, the young turtles dig their way out of the sand and try to quickly find their way to the sea. Ocean currents carry them out into the open ocean. The young turtles are lucky if they survive to adulthood, because many predators on land and in the sea like to eat them. These predators include foxes, raccoons, crabs, fish, and seabirds.

Threats. Human activities have caused a dramatic decline in the population of Kemp's ridley sea turtles. In 1947, an estimated 42,000 Kemp's ridley females were observed in one arribada near Rancho Nuevo. By the late 1970's, the largest arribada consisted of only about 200 females. Scientists blame this population crash on two main factors. Many of the sea turtles were killed when they became caught accidentally in large commercial fishing nets—especially shrimp trawls—and other fishing gear. In addition, people routinely collected the turtles' eggs and hunted the turtles for their meat.

Kemp's ridley sea turtles and other sea turtles are now protected by international agreements. Arribada sizes of Kemp's ridleys have steadily increased since about the year 2000.

Although the Kemp's ridley sea turtle is protected by international agreement, the trade in their eggs and meat continues illegally.

Caretta caretta

Conservation status: Endangered

Loggerhead sea turtles—also called loggerheads—were named for their unusually large heads. The heads have boney, parrotlike "beaks." Their jaws are capable of crushing marine animals with even hard, thick shells, including such snails as whelks and conches. Loggerhead turtles are about 3 feet (1 meter) long and weigh about 250 pounds (113 kilograms). Their *carapace* (top shell) is reddish-brown and shaped somewhat like a heart.

Habitats. Loggerheads are widespread throughout the tropical and *temperate* (between arctic and tropical) waters of the Atlantic, Pacific, and Indian oceans, as well as the Mediterranean Sea. There are more loggerheads in U.S. coastal waters than any other kind of sea turtle. Loggerheads migrate vast distances between feeding and nesting areas. Some populations of these turtles regularly cross the Pacific Ocean between nesting beaches in Japan and feeding sites off the coast of Mexico—a distance of more than 7,500 miles (12,000 kilometers).

More than 80 percent of loggerhead nesting beaches are along the eastern coast of the United States, the coast of Oman (on the Arabian Peninsula), and the northwestern and northeastern coasts of Australia (including the Great Barrier Reef, the world's largest system of coral reefs). A female may nest three to five times over a three-month breeding season, during which she may lay more than 35 pounds (16 kilograms) of eggs.

Threats. As with most sea turtles, the greatest threat to loggerheads is being caught and trapped accidentally in large fishing nets. The turtles are also caught and killed for their meat and body parts, mainly in Central America and Mexico. The most important protected site for loggerheads is Archie Carr National Wildlife Refuge on Florida's east coast, where biologists typically count more than 10,000 loggerhead nests each year.

The loggerhead sea turtle is often trapped and killed in large fishing nets.

Chelonia mydas

Conservation status: Endangered

These turtles get their name from the color of the fat in their body. The fat turns green from the green seaweed and other algae that they eat. The green sea turtle is the only marine turtle that eats only vegetation.

Green sea turtle

Appearance. Green sea turtles are one of the heaviest sea turtles. The 3.5-foot- (1-meter-) long body of an adult may tip the scales at 400 pounds (180 kilograms). But newly hatched green sea turtles are just about 2 inches (5 centimeters) long and weigh only about 0.9 ounce (25 grams).

Habitat. This *species* (type) is found in oceans throughout the world, most commonly in tropical and subtropical regions. Their largest nesting sites are on Costa Rica's Caribbean coast and the Great Barrier Reef. Roughly 20,000 females nest there each year.

Threats. Besides being threatened by capture in fishing nets and the hunting of adults and eggs, green sea turtles suffer from a disease called fibropapillomatosis. Turtles with this disease have large growths that interfere with their ability to swim, see, and eat.

The green sea turtle is the only marine turtle that eats only vegetation.

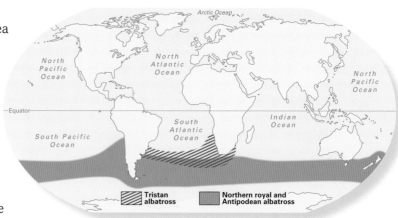

Albatrosses are large, mostly white sea birds that are found over nearly all oceans, except the North Atlantic. The largest *species* (type) of albatross—the great albatross—belongs to the *genus Diomedea*. (A genus is a group of related species.) Some of these big birds, including the wandering albatross and the southern royal albatross, have wingspans of 11 feet (3.3 meters) or greater. That is the longest wingspan of any living bird.

Food and reproduction. Albatrosses feed on fish, squid, *crustaceans* (hard-shelled animals), and other animals that they grab from the ocean surface with their long bills. The birds also sometimes follow fishing ships, waiting for the crews to toss the waste parts of marine creatures killed for food, called offal, into the water. Albatrosses may fly thousands of miles over the sea as they search for food.

About the only time that albatrosses come to land is to breed. Then huge groups of females nest together on remote islands. Each female lays one white egg on bare ground or in a shallow nest. The hatchling has dark fluffy down feathers. The birds become increasingly white as they age. Most adult albatrosses are all white except for their dark upper wings.

Tristan albatross
Diomedea dabbenena

Conservation status: Critically Endangered

The Tristan albatross is one of the most seriously endangered albatross species. It used to be classified as a wandering albatross until scientists determined that it is a separate species. Tristan albatrosses are a little smaller than wandering albatrosses. They also take a longer time to get their adult white plumage.

Tristan albatrosses are named after the Tristan da Cunha group, islands in the South Atlantic Ocean between Africa and South

America. The birds formerly bred in large numbers on these islands, which are some of the most remote islands in the world. Today, the birds are found mainly on one island in this group, called Gough Island. Biologists estimate that the albatross population on Gough has decreased by about 30 percent since the mid-1900's. And the bird's numbers continue to fall.

The Tristan albatross population has dropped for two main reasons. The eggs and chicks are eaten by *feral* pigs and cats

(domestic animals that escaped into the wild), as well as rats and mice introduced to the Tristan da Cunha islands by people. In addition, the birds are sometimes caught and killed accidentally on *longlines* (commercial fishing lines that carry thousands of baited hooks).

Antipodean albatross
Diomedea antipodensis
Conservation status: Vulnerable

Northern royal albatross
Diomedea sanfordi
Conservation status: Endangered

The Antipodean albatross and northern royal albatross are two other species threatened with extinction. The Antipodean albatross breeds on the Antipodes Islands, Auckland Islands,

Like other albatrosses, the northern royal albatross (above) and Tristan albatross (opposite page) spend most of their life soaring over the sea, coming to land only to breed.

and Chatham Islands—all southeast of New Zealand. The northern royal albatross breeds on South Island (one of the two major islands that make up New Zealand) and the Chatham and Auckland islands. Nonnative animals have killed many northern royal albatross eggs and chicks. These animals include cats, pigs, mice, and a kind of weasel called a stoat. Flies that lay their eggs in animal flesh, called blowflies, also attack the birds and their chicks. The albatrosses are also often caught on longlines set out for commercial fish.

Rockhopper penguin
Eudyptes chrysocome

Conservation status: Vulnerable

Northern rockhopper (Moseley's) penguin
Eudyptes moseleyi

Conservation status: Endangered

Rockhopper penguins are short penguins with long, spiky, black-and-yellow feathers on the top of their head. They're only about 20 inches (51 centimeters) tall and weigh about 5 pounds (2.3 kilograms). They are quite colorful, with blood-red eyes, reddish-orange beaks, and pink feet. Rockhopper penguins live in the sea and on islands north of Antarctica—including the Falkland

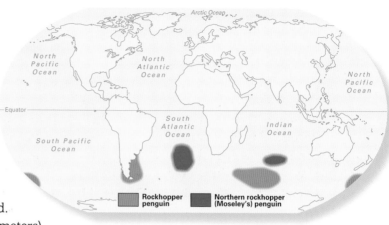

Islands near Chile and islands south of New Zealand. The northern rockhopper is found mostly on the Tristan da Cunha islands, between Africa and South America.

Social life. These little penguins are very social birds. During the annual breeding season, the birds leave their ocean feeding areas to come together in huge colonies on land. The largest colonies have hundreds of thousands of birds, making a rockhopper colony a very noisy place. The birds return to the same nesting sites each year. Biologists have discovered—by putting identification tags on the birds—that the male and female of a mating pair usually try to find each other year after year on the nesting grounds.

Caring for the young. The female lays one or two eggs. The parents spend about a month taking turns incubating the eggs by pressing them against a warm, bare spot of skin at the bottom of their belly. Any other penguin that gets too close to the eggs is likely to be pecked by the parent. After the young penguins hatch, the father takes care of them, while the mother goes back to sea to get food for the chicks.

Rockhopper penguins, which sport spiky, black-and-yellow feathers on their head, nest only on islands north of Antarctica.

After about 25 days, the chicks leave the nest and join groups of other chicks their age.

Grooming. Rockhopper penguins groom one another and themselves. During grooming, the penguin takes a waxy substance from a gland near its tail and uses its beak to spread the substance over the body feathers. This activity smoothes out the feathers and keeps them waterproof, so that seawater does not make the penguin's skin wet and cold.

Fishing. Rockhopper penguins usually stay close to the shore when they're out at sea. But they sometimes dive as deep as 330 feet (100 meters) in search of food. Their main prey are fish and squid as well as *krill* (shrimplike animals) and other *crustaceans* (hard-shelled animals). When they're on land and not nesting, the penguins usually move by leaping across the rocky landscape. Unlike most penguins, they do not waddle when they walk.

Threats. Rockhopper penguins are more numerous than most other penguins. However, their numbers are declining fast. Populations of the fish and squid that they eat have been depleted by commercial fishing operations. Some penguins get caught in commercial fishing nets. Pollution has contaminated their food and their *habitats* (living places). On some islands, cats, rats, pigs, and other predators introduced by people eat the eggs and chicks of the penguins. Scientists believe that the penguins and their habitats may also be harmed by *climate change* (warming of Earth's atmosphere).

Enhydra lutris

Conservation status: Endangered

Sea otters are marine members of the weasel family. They live in the North Pacific Ocean near the shores of Siberia and western North America, from the Aleutian Islands to Baja California.

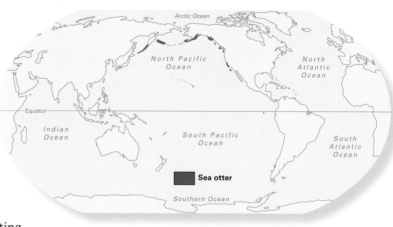

Sea otters hardly ever leave the water. They even eat and sleep while floating on their back, often in large groups. To stay in one place while floating at the surface, the otters sometimes anchor themselves to large seaweed called kelp. Females give birth in the water. As a mother sea otter paddles about on her back, she carries her pup on her chest.

Appearance. Most sea otters grow from 4 to 5 feet (1.2 to 1.5 meters) long and weigh from 60 to 85 pounds (27 to 39 kilograms). Their bodies have many *adaptations* (useful traits) that help them thrive in their watery homes. Their back feet are *webbed* (have tissue between the toes) so they can push against water like flippers. Otters also have thick, brown, water-repellent fur. The fur keeps seawater off the skin so that it stays dry and warm. Other aquatic adaptations are nostrils and ears that close when otters are underwater.

Eating. Sea otters can dive as deep as 180 feet (55 meters) for food and stay underwater for as long as four minutes. They eat a variety of animals, including such *mollusks* (soft-bodied animals) as clams, mussels, octopuses, and squid, as well as crabs, sea urchins, fish. And they eat a lot—as much as one-fifth of their body weight every day.

Sea otters are fascinating to watch as they eat, especially when they open the hard shells of clams or mussels to get at the soft meat inside. To do this, a sea otter uses its front paws like hands, to grasp and hold the mollusk. It may try to pry open the shell with its paws and teeth. If that doesn't work, it may pound one clam or mussel against another. But the most interesting way that a sea otter opens a shell is by diving down to the seafloor to grab a rock, coming back to the surface to float on its back, balancing the rock on its belly, and hammering the shellfish against the rock until the shell breaks open.

Threats. The coats of sea otters are thicker than the coat of any other mammal—with 645,000 hairs per square inch (100,000 hairs per square centimeter). This thick, beautiful fur led humans to hunt sea otters for hundreds of years. From the mid-1700's through the 1800's, fur traders killed so many sea otters that the *species* (type) almost became extinct.

In 1911, Canada, Japan, Russia, and the United States signed a treaty that banned the hunting of sea otters. As a result, the sea otter population has increased from fewer than 2,000 to more than 100,000 today. However, the species is still threatened by diseases, oil spills and other pollution, and human developments along coastlines.

A mother sea otter with a baby nestled on her chest floats on the waters of Prince William Bay in Alaska.

Northern fur seal

Callorhinus ursinus

Conservation status: Vulnerable

The northern fur seal is a large member of the "eared seal" family. Eared seals, which also include sea lions, have flaps that cover their ear openings. Other *pinnipeds* (the group made up of seals, sea lions, and walruses) have uncovered ear openings. Eared seals also have front flippers that are long and flat and hind flippers that can be rotated forward and down to walk on land. The animals use all four flippers to walk. But they swim using only their front flippers. The seals also have slitlike nostrils, which they can close underwater.

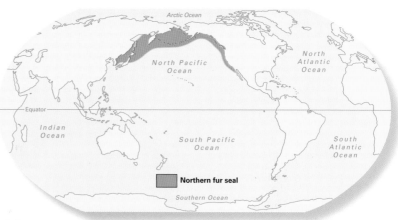

Size. Male and female eared seals differ from each other in size much more than the males and females of most other kinds of mammals do. When the two sexes of a *species* (type) have great physical differences, the species is said to be sexually dimorphic. A male northern fur seal can grow to a length of 7 feet (2 meters) and a weight of 600 pounds (270 kilograms), but females are no longer than 5 feet (1.5 meters) and no heavier than 130 pounds (60 kilograms). Males also have much larger necks, shoulders, and chests than females do.

The brown, black, or gray fur of northern fur seals is very dense, with 297,000 hairs per square inch (46,000 hairs per square centimeter). This thick fur covers the entire body except for the flippers. Males have darker fur than that of the females.

Habitat. Northern fur seals live throughout the North Pacific Ocean, from California in the United States to Japan. They eat mainly fish and squid that they catch in the sea. They can dive deeper and stay underwater longer than most other mammals, because their bodies store more oxygen. Fur seals can store twice as much oxygen as human beings can. They often stay out at sea for many days before returning to land. Adults typically spend about 300 days per year at sea.

Breeding. In summer, northern fur seals breed on rocky or sandy beaches on U.S. and Russian islands in the North Pacific Ocean and Bering Sea. About half of all northern fur seals breed on the Pribilof Islands off the coast of mainland Alaska. Their breeding sites are called rookeries. Males arrive at the rookeries first and set up territories for themselves. Females arrive later and select a mate. A female gives birth to only one pup each breeding season. The pups of many females play and sleep together in large groups called pods. A mother can identify her pup by the calls it makes and by its scent.

Threats. Northern fur seals were hunted to the brink of extinction—mainly for their fur—until an international agreement in 1911 banned the commercial hunting of the species at sea. But the agreement allowed hunting on land. Since the 1970's, the demand for seal fur has declined as people have become more concerned about the welfare of the animals. Commercial hunting of the fur seals on the Pribilof Islands stopped in 1986. However, native people of Alaska are allowed to kill hundreds of the seals each year to meet their needs.

Female northern fur seals crowd together in a *rookery* (breeding site) on St. Paul's Island in Alaska.

Dugong

Dugong dugon

Conservation status: Vulnerable

The dugong is a large *herbivorous* (plant-eating) mammal that lives its whole life in the sea. To breathe, it pokes its nostrils above the water to draw in air. The dugong is one of four *species* (types) in a group called Sirenia. The other three species are manatees. The word *siren* means *a beautiful but dangerous woman.* Some historians believe this name was given to the dugong-manatee group because stories told in ancient times by sailors who saw these animals at the sea surface led to the myths about mermaids. The animals are also known as "sea cows."

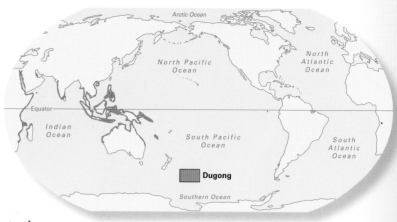

Dugong

Habitat. Dugongs live in the shallow, warm waters of the Indian and South Pacific oceans along coastlines. Their *range* (area in which they occur naturally) extends from eastern Africa to northern Australia, Papua New Guinea, and other Pacific islands. Dugongs eat seagrasses (the only flowering plants that grow in the ocean) and algae, using their flippers to push the vegetation into their mouth. Sometimes they grab the plant with their bristly upper lip and yank it, ripping the whole plant out of the sea floor.

Appearance. The average length of an adult dugong is about 9 feet (2.7 meters). It weighs about 600 pounds (270 kilograms). However, some individuals are as long as 13 feet (4 meters) and may weigh as much as 1 ton (0.9 metric ton). Both males and females have two tusks in their upper jaw. The female's tusks cannot be seen on the outside because they are too small. A male may sometimes use his long tusks to pull plants from the sea floor.

A female dugong typically gives birth to one calf every three to seven years. A calf may stay with its mother for two years. Dugongs can live to be more than 70 years old.

Threats. Dugong numbers have fallen for several reasons. People have hunted the animals for hundreds of years for their meat and oil (obtained from their fat). Such hunting is now regulated by laws, especially in Australia. But limited hunting of dugongs by the Aboriginal (native) People of Australia is allowed because it is important to the traditional culture of these people. The animals also provide protein for the Aborigines, many of whom live in remote places where fresh food is difficult to find.

The shallow sea *habitat* (living place) of dugongs has been damaged by human settlements along coasts. Dangerous chemicals from farms and cities pollute the water. The amount of *silt* (sand, soil, and other small particles) washing into the water has increased along the coasts as a result of construction, farming, and deforestation. The silt smothers seagrass beds. The busy boat traffic in some areas leads to collisions with dugongs. Some dugongs drown after getting trapped in commercial fishing nets.

Conservation. Dugongs are protected in Australian waters. However, their slow reproduction rate means that even protected populations will take a long time to recover.

Dugongs are threatened by hunting, fishing, water pollution, and such activities as farming, construction, and deforestation.

West Indian manatee
Trichechus manatus
Conservation status: Vulnerable

West African manatee
Trichechus senegalensis
Conservation status: Vulnerable

Amazonian manatee
Trichechus inunguis
Conservation status: Vulnerable

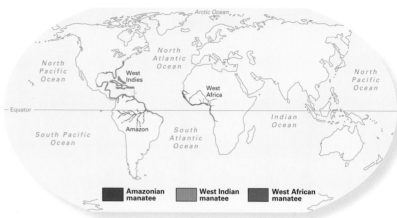

Manatees are large *herbivorous* (plant-eating) mammals related to dugongs. The West Indian manatee lives near islands in the Caribbean Sea and along coasts and in rivers from the mid-Atlantic Ocean and southeastern United States to northeastern Brazil. The West African manatee lives in the rivers and coastal waters of West Africa. The Amazonian manatee is the only manatee that does not live in the ocean. It is found only in South American rivers.

Manatees and dugongs. Manatees have a rounded, paddlelike tail, while dugongs have a triangular, whalelike tail. Unlike dugongs, manatees do not have tusks in their upper jaws. Most manatees are larger than dugongs. Manatees may be about 13 feet (4 meters) long and weigh more than 1.7 tons (1.6 metric tons). In addition, manatees can live in fresh water rivers as well as salty seas. The dugong must live in saltwater.

Characteristics. Manatees have several traits that are unusual for mammals. Their skeletons are made of solid bone, with no soft tissue, called marrow, inside. As a result, their skeletons are very heavy. A manatee's lungs are unique in the way they spread horizontally along the body. The teeth are unique because they consist only of grinding teeth called molars. The molars are replaced as they wear out.

Food. The manatee eats a greater variety of vegetation than the dugong does, including algae, seagrasses, and even onshore plants that they grab from the water. A 1,000-pound (450-kilogram) manatee can eat 100 pounds (45 kilograms) of food in a single day.

Reproduction. During the breeding season, manatees gather in large herds. Each herd has many males but only one female. Several males surround the female, who usually mates with more than one of them. A female typically gives birth to one calf every two to three years. She cares for the calf for one to two years. Calves *nurse* (drink milk) underwater, from nipples behind the mother's flippers. They begin to feed on vegetation after a few weeks. Mothers and calves communicate by squeaking and grunting.

Threats. All three manatee *species* (types) are threatened with extinction. They have long been overhunted for their meat and the oil derived from their fat. Their coastal *habitats* (living places) have been destroyed or *degraded* (decreased in quality) by human activities, including pollution and *silt* (sand, soil, and other matter in water) from construction, farming, and urban developments. The animals are also killed in accidents with boats and trapped in commercial fishing nets. In Florida, a fast-growing human population threatens the natural springs that supply manatee wetland habitats.

The African manatee (left) and West Indian manatee (below) as well as the Amazonian manatee have long been hunted for their meat and the oil derived from their fat.

Balaenoptera musculus

Conservation status: Endangered

The blue whale is one of the largest animals that has ever lived. It grows up to 100 feet (30 meters) long and can weigh more than 150 tons (136 metric tons). That's as heavy as about 30 African elephants. A blue whale's heart is as big as a car, and its main blood vessel is big enough for a person to crawl through. The animal's name comes from its speckled, bluish-gray skin. Blue whales can live for 80 years or more.

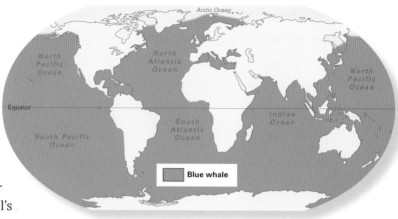

Blue whale

Feeding. The blue whale is a type of baleen whale. Such whales have hundreds of thin, fringed plates, called *baleen*, hanging from each side of the upper jaw. The baleen works like a filter as the whales feed. The blue whale feeds by opening its mouth and swimming through masses of *krill* (shrimplike animals) and other kinds of tiny drifting creatures called zooplankton. Tons of water and zooplankton flow into the whale's mouth. The whale then closes its mouth and squirts the water out through the baleen, trapping the food inside.

Swimming. Blue whales swim fast, reaching speeds as great as 31 miles (50 kilometers) per hour. The whales surface to breathe three to six times in rapid succession, then dive for several minutes. When they swim to the surface to breathe, they make loud noises as the air bursts from their nostrils, called blowholes. The spout—the mixture of air and water—from the exhalation can rise up to 30 feet (9 meters).

Communication. Members of this *species* (type) communicate with one another with low, moanlike calls. Many of their calls are so low that they are below the range of human hearing. These calls can travel for hundreds of miles through the sea, allowing blue whales to stay in contact with one another when they are widely separated.

Habitat. Blue whales live in all the oceans. They feed in cool waters near the North and South poles during the warmer months. As winter and the breeding season approach, the whales migrate to warm waters closer to the equator, the imaginary line around the middle of Earth. The female blue whale gives birth to a single calf, which comes out of the mother measuring about 23 feet (7 meters) in length.

Threats. Because of their great size, fast speed, and remote polar feeding sites, blue whales were not widely hunted before the mid-1800's. At that time, however, powerful harpoon-firing cannons mounted on the decks of boats made it easier for commercial whalers to catch blue whales. The animals were killed to get their meat, their oil (for lamps, perfume, and other items), and their baleen (to make into umbrella ribs, buggy whips, hair brushes, and other products).

By the mid-1900's, blue whales had been hunted nearly to extinction. However, their numbers have steadily increased since the 1960's, after many countries agreed to stop or limit the hunting of the species.

Hunted nearly to extinction, blue whales have grown more numerous since the 1960's because of laws that forbid or severely limit their killing.

North Atlantic right whale
Eubalaena glacialis
Conservation status: Endangered

North Pacific right whale
Eubalaena japonica
Conservation status: Endangered

Southern right whale
Eubalaena australis
Conservation status: Least Concern

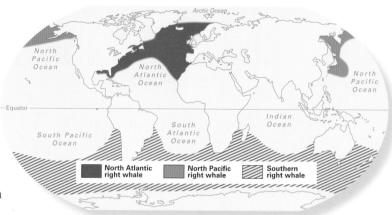

Right whales are *baleen* whales with huge heads. Baleen are thin, fringed plates that hang from each side of the upper jaw. The right whale's head typically makes up a third of its body, which is about 50 feet (15 meters) long. The baleen plates may be as long as 8 feet (2.4 meters). Right whales are mostly dark gray or black. Patches of rough, white skin on the head are caused by parasites known as whale lice.

Habitat. Northern right whales live in the *temperate* (between arctic and tropical) seas of the Northern Hemisphere, with one *species* (type) found in the North Atlantic and one in the North Pacific. The southern right whale lives in the temperate waters of the Southern Hemisphere. Like other baleen whales, right whales feed mainly on tiny, floating creatures called zooplankton.

Communication. Right whales sometimes breach, or jump out of the water. They also slap the sea surface with their tails or fins. Many scientists suspect that these actions may be forms of communication. Right whales also produce low groans and moans, which can travel long distances through the ocean. Scientists do not understand the exact meanings of these calls.

Whale hunting. Today, right whales are among the rarest of all whales. Whalers about 800 years ago named these animals *right* whales, because they considered them the right whale to hunt. Right whales are relatively easy to hunt because they swim slowly and close to shore. In addition, dead right whales float because their bodies have so much *blubber*

A North Atlantic right whale breaches, leaping from the water and then splashing back in. The whales may breach to communicate, to rid their bodies of parasites, or just for fun.

(fat), which is lighter than water. Their blubber layer is about 20 inches (50 centimeters) thick. People obtained oil from the blubber, which was used in lamps and perfumes. They used the baleen to make clothing, umbrellas, buggy whips, hairbrushes, and many other items. From the 1600's through the 1800's, whalers slaughtered so many right whales that the animals almost became extinct.

Threats. Scientists estimate that the total right whale population today is several thousand. Although they are protected against hunting, the animals continue to face threats—mainly getting hit by ships or trapped in fishing nets. Another problem is pollution of their coastal *habitats* (living areas).

The long-distance communication system of right whales and several other types of whales and dolphins is disturbed by sonar systems used in military exercises by the United States Navy. These systems use sound to make measurements and identify underwater objects. The sonar seems to confuse and frighten the whales, causing them to perform abnormal behaviors. Some whales stop eating or try to escape the sounds by *beaching* themselves (swimming onto shore), where they die.

Conservation. Right whales have been protected by international law since the 1930's, but their numbers have not rebounded very much. The species reproduces slowly. Females cannot reproduce until they are about 10 years old. A pregnant female carries one developing calf in her body for about a year before giving birth. She typically has only one calf every three years.

Sperm whale

Physeter macrocephalus

Conservation status: Vulnerable

The sperm whale is the largest toothed whale. Other types of toothed whales are dolphins, porpoises, belugas, and narwhals. Only certain *species* (types) of *baleen* whales, such as blue whales, are larger. Baleen whales have hundreds of thin, fringed plates hanging from each side of the upper jaw. Male sperm whales grow to a length of about 60 feet (18 meters); females grow to about 40 feet (12 meters).

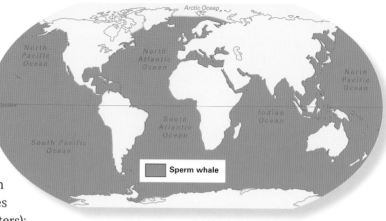

Appearance. Sperm whales range in color from brownish-black to dark gray. They have a low hump on their back and several ridges between their hump and tail. A sperm whale's head makes up about a third of the animal's body length. The head contains the largest brain of any animal. A male sperm whale's brain weighs about 17 pounds (7.8 kilograms).

This big brain does not mean that sperm whales are more intelligent than other animals—though they are intelligent. Their brain is large because their body is large. The head is filled with an oily substance, called spermaceti, that people once used for making candles, and sperm oil, which was used as a lubricant for making machine parts work smoothly.

Feeding. Sperm whales use their toothed mouth to capture squid and fish. There are from 20 to 26 large cone-shaped teeth on each side of the lower jaw. The upper jaw has only tiny teeth or no teeth at all. The whales may dive deeper than 3,300 feet (1,000 meters) in search of prey. They can remain underwater for more than an hour. When they surface, they breathe air through a single blowhole on the left front of the head.

Families. Female sperm whales typically give birth to one calf every five years. The newborn calf is usually about 13 feet (4 meters) long. Family groups are usually made up of approximately 12 adult females and their calves. When the males are between 4 and 20 years old, they leave these family groups to form "bachelor schools," which are groups of males about the same age. Eventually, those male groups break up. Large adult males typically live alone.

Habitat. Sperm whales live in all the world's oceans. Adult males swim north or south to cooler waters in spring. Females and young whales stay in groups in or near tropical seas all year.

Threats. Sperm whales were hunted so relentlessly in the 1800's and 1900's—mainly for their meat and spermaceti—that they almost became extinct. Whalers killed an estimated 1 million of the animals. People also killed the whales to get a waxy substance called ambergris, which forms inside their intestines. Ambergris used to be valued for flavoring food and because it made perfume scents last longer. In the 1980's, the International Whaling Commission (an international organization that sets rules for whaling) banned most hunting of sperm whales. However, some whales are killed by collisions with ships or die while trapped in large fishnets.

A sperm whale mother and her calf swim through the Caribbean Sea.

Glossary

Adaptation A characteristic of an organism that makes it better able to survive and reproduce in its environment.

Arribada The mass arrival of female sea turtles on a nesting beach.

Baleen Thin, fringed plates that hang from the upper sides of a baleen whale's mouth and work like a filter to catch small animals from sea water.

Beach Regarding marine animals, to swim onto shore and become stranded.

Biologically diverse Containing a wide variety of plant or animal life.

Bivalve A mollusk with a shell made of two pieces that are connected at one end with a hinge that allows the shell to open.

Bleaching The process in which corals turn white and die when the food-producing algae that live in their tissues die; it is related to the warming of ocean waters.

Blubber A thick layer of fat that lies under the skin and over the muscles of some sea animals.

Carapace The top shell of an animal.

Cartilage Tissue that is softer and more flexible than bone.

Climate change Also known as global warming; an increase in the average temperature at Earth's surface since the mid-1800's, caused mainly by human activities.

Crustacean An invertebrate animal with many jointed legs and a hard external shell.

Degraded To be reduced in quality.

Dorsal fin A fin on the back of a fish or whale.

Ecosystem A natural system made up of living organisms and their physical environment.

Ecotourist A person who travels to see wildlife and natural environments, trying not to harm those environments.

Exoskeleton A hard, external covering or other structure that protects or supports an animal's body.

Feral Refers to domestic animals that have escaped into the wild.

Fossil fuel Coal, natural gas, and other energy-providing material formed from the long-dead remains of living things.

Genus A group of related species.

Gill A breathing organ in fish and other animals.

Habitat The kind of place in which an organism usually lives.

Herbivorous Feeding on plants.

Invertebrate An animal without a backbone.

Iridescent Displaying changing colors, like those of the rainbow, depending on the angle viewed from.

Krill A small, shrimplike crustacean that is eaten by many whales and other marine animals.

Larva The immature form of an animal (plural is larvae).

Longline A long commercial fishing line that carries thousands of baited hooks.

Mollusks A group of soft-bodied invertebrates.

Mutualism Any relationship between two different species in which both species benefit.

Notochord A hollow, fluid-filled rod under the spinal cord of early and relatively simple vertebrates.

Pheromone A chemical substance released by certain animal species to affect the behavior or development of other members of the species.

Photosynthesis The process by which plants and algae make carbohydrate food from carbon dioxide and water in the presence of light, releasing oxygen as a by-product.

Pinnipeds The biological group made up of seals, sea lions, and walruses.

Polyp A water animal that consists largely of a stomach and a mouth with fingerlike tentacles to gather in food.

Pores Openings.

Purse seining A commercial fishing method in which large nets are used to encircle the fish.

Range The district in which certain plants or animals live or naturally occur.

Rostrum The snout of a sawfish that is lined with sharp scales resembling teeth.

Sessile Fixed to one place.

Silt Sand, soil, and other small particles from the land that enter bodies of water.

Spawn To lay eggs.

Species A group of animals or plants that have certain permanent characteristics in common and are able to interbreed.

Stag A male deer.

Temperate Region of the ocean between tropical and polar regions.

Toxic Poisonous.

Vertebrate An animal with a backbone.

Warm-blooded Maintaining the same body temperature, regardless of the warmth of an animal's surroundings.

Webbed Having skin joining the toes.

Zooxanthellae Single-celled algae.

Books

Dembicki, Matt. *Wild Ocean: Sharks, Whales, Rays, and Other Endangered Sea Creatures.* Golden, CO: Fulcrum, 2014. Print.

Hammond, Paula. *The Atlas of Endangered Animals: Wildlife Under Threat Around the World.* Tarrytown, NY: Marshall Cavendish, 2010. Print.

Hoare, Ben, and Tom Jackson. *Endangered Animals.* New York: DK Pub., 2010. Print.

Silhol, Sandrine, Gaëlle Guérive, and Marie Doucedame. *Extraordinary Endangered Animals.* New York: Abrams Books for Young Readers, 2011. Print.

Swinburne, Stephen R. *Sea Turtle Scientist.* Boston: Houghton Mifflin Harcourt, 2014. Print.

Websites

Arkive. Wildscreen, 2014. Web. 14 May 2014.

"Especies Fact Sheets." *Kids' Planet.* Defenders of Wildlife, n.d. Web. 14 May 2014.

NOAA Ocean Today. National Ocean Service, 2014. Web. 14 May 2014.

"The Ocean: Marine Protected Areas." *National Geographic.* National Geographic Society, 2014. Web. 14 May 2014.

"Photogallery: Marine Species Under Threat." *National Geographic.* National Geographic Society, 2014. Web. 14 May 2014.

Smithsonian Ocean Portal. Smithsonian Institution, 2013. Web. 14 May 14, 2014.

Organizations *for helping endangered animals*

Alaska Wildlife Adoption
By adopting an animal at the Alaska Wildlife Conservation Center, you can enjoy animal parenthood without all the work.
http://www.alaskawildlife.org/support/alaska-wildlife-adoption/

Defenders of Wildlife
Founded in 1947, Defenders of Wildlife is a major national conservation organization focused on wildlife and habitat conservation.
http://www.defenders.org/take-action

National Geographic – Big Cats Initiative
National Geographic, along with Dereck and Beverly Joubert, launched the Big Cats Initiative to raise awareness and implement change to the dire situation facing big cats.
http://animals.nationalgeographic.com/animals/big-cats-initiative/

National Geographic – The Ocean Initiative
National Geographic's Ocean Initiative helps identify and support individuals and organizations that are using creative and entrepreneurial approaches to marine conservation.
http://ocean.nationalgeographic.com/ocean/about-ocean-initiative/

National Wildlife Federation – Adoption Center
Symbolically adopt your favorite species and at the same time support the National Wildlife Federation's important work protecting wildlife and connecting people to nature.
http://www.shopnwf.org/Adoption-Center/index.cat

Neighbor Ape
Neighbor Ape strives to conserve the habitat of wild chimpanzees in southeastern Senegal, to protect the chimpanzees themselves, and to provide for the well-being of the Senegalese people who have traditionally lived in the area alongside these chimpanzees.
http://www.globalgiving.org/donate/10235/neighbor-ape/

Smithsonian National Zoo – Adopt a Species
The Adopt a Species program supports the National Zoo's extraordinary work in the conservation and care of the world's rarest animals.
http://nationalzoo.si.edu/support/adoptspecies/

World Wildlife Fund
World Wildlife Fund works in 100 countries and is supported by over 1 million members in the United States and close to 5 million globally.
http://www.worldwildlife.org/how-to-help

Index

Acknowledgments

The publishers acknowledge the following sources for illustrations. Credits read from top to bottom, left to right, on their respective pages. All maps, charts, and diagrams were prepared by the staff unless otherwise noted.

COVER © Scubazoo/Alamy Images; © Andrea Matone, Alamy Images
4 © Andrea Matone, Alamy Images
7 © Image Broker/SuperStock
8 © RGB Ventures/SuperStock/Alamy Images
9 © Helmut Corneli, Alamy Images
11 © Roberto Rinaldi, Minden Pictures
13 © VPC Travel Photo/Alamy Images; © Sea Pics
15 © Shutterstock
17 © Mark Conlin, VWPics/Alamy Images
18 © Martin Strmiska, Alamy Images
20 © Yves Lanceau, Oceans-Image/Photoshot
21 © Vision/Alamy Images
23 © Michael Patrick O'Neill, Alamy Images; © Mark Conlin, Alamy Images
25-26 © Michael Patrick O'Neill, Alamy Images
27 © Mint Images/SuperStock
28 © Tui De Roy, Minden Pictures
29 © Ray Wilson, Alamy Images
30 © Chris Howarth, South Atlantic/Alamy Images
31 © Kevin Schafer, Minden Pictures
33 © Steven J. Kazlowski, Alamy Images
35 © Alaska Stock/Alamy Images
37 © Martin Strmiska, Alamy Images
39 © Tsuneo Nakamura, Volvox/Alamy Images
39 © Brandon Cole, Alamy Images
41 © Francois Gohier, VWPics/Alamy Images
42 © Brian J. Skerry, National Geographic Creative
44 © Reinhard Dirscherl, Alamy Images